PEACE
in the
Valley

PEACE
in the
Valley

DEVOTIONS FOR THE HOSPICE PATIENT

KAY SINGLEY

ARPress
ILLUMINATING IDEAS
EMPOWERING VOICES

ARPress
45 Dan Road Suite 5
Canton MA 02021
Hotline: 1(888) 821-0229
Fax: 1(508) 545-7580

Ordering Information:
Quantity sales. Special discounts are available on quantity purchases by corporations, associations, and others. For details, contact the publisher at the address above.

Printed in the United States of America.

ISBN-13:   Softcover   979-8-89330-202-8
                  eBook   979-8-89330-203-5

Library of Congress Control Number: 2024900836

Table of Contents

Acknowledgements

To my family for their encouragement and support in this endeavor.

Dedication

In memory of my husband, Rob, my parents, and all of my hospice patients who have taught me so much.

Peace in the Valley

"Yea, though I walk through the valley of the shadow of death, I will fear no evil: for thou art with me; thy rod and thy staff they comfort me." Psalm 23:4

A million thoughts tumble over each other in your mind, yet you can't speak one of them. The doctor has told you and your family that your days of life on the earth are numbered. You are afraid - mainly of the unknown. You long for peace.

David, the Psalmist of the Bible, had times when he felt that he was walking through the valley of the shadow of death. How did he handle that? He handled it with faith and trust in God who created him. David says that he will not fear because God is with him. He is comforted.

God knows the answers to all of your questions. He has been to all of the places and in all of the circumstances that are unknown to you. God is faithful to those who have placed trust in Him.

God has made a way for every soul that He has created to return to Him. God, in His great love for humankind, sent His Son, Jesus Christ, into the world. Jesus took upon Himself the punishment for human sin, which is death. We need to recognize that Christ substituted for us on the cross so that we could have fellowship with God forever. When we ask Christ to forgive our sins and live in our heart, He brings a peace to our soul that passes all understanding.

A small child, who is afraid of the dark, will enter a dark room holding onto a beloved parent's hand. God is that loving parent for all the children that He has created. There is no fear in His presence. He truly brings peace to your soul as you travel through the valley of the shadow of death. God brings His weary child to Heaven where there is peace forever. God loves all of His children. He offers peace to all who will trust in Him. Won't you trust God to bring you peace in your valley?

Prayer: Dear Heavenly Father, It is hard to accept this sudden change in my life. Yet, I give You my fear of the unknown, trusting that You are able to care for me as I travel through the valley of the shadow of death. I believe that Jesus is God's Son and I ask Him to forgive my past sins. Please, Jesus, come to live in my heart. I now claim God's promise of eternal life forever in Heaven because I have trusted in Christ as my Savior. I thank You for the peace that You will bring me daily, in Jesus' name, I pray. Amen.

Why?

"Trust in the Lord, with all thine heart; and lean not unto thine own understanding." Proverbs 3:5

In times like these, many questions that come to your mind may be prefaced by the word, "why". Why did this happen to me? Why am I not getting well? Why doesn't God do something?

You find that there is not a human answer to any of these "why" questions that will satisfy. "Why" is a question asked but never answered in the Bible. Only God can minister to these "why" questions. Yet, He may not even give you an answer. But, He is able to give you the comfort of His presence if you will allow Him to do so. Trusting God is the way we open the door to His comfort.

What is trust? Isn't it allowing God to care for us when we don't understand His will for us? Trusting God is giving up our will and our wants. We let God have His way whatever it is. Yet, may we remember that God always wants to bring good things to our lives. Could it be that He has something better for you than days of endless pain and illness? Could it be that He would like to give you peace, freedom from sickness, and the home of Heaven? Perhaps, He desires to fellowship with you. The Bible teaches us that to be absent from the body is to be present with the Lord. To be present with the Lord is the hope of every believer. This is the ultimate goal of a life of faith. God will bring His best to those who trust Him.

Prayer: O God, help me trust You with my body, soul and mind. Help me rest in the fact that You will bring good to me even in this. Let me feel Your presence and Your comfort. Thank you for Your love, in Jesus' name, I pray. Amen.

I've Never Been Religious

"Jesus saith unto him, I am the way, the truth, and the life: no man cometh unto the Father, but by me." John 14:6

"I've never been religious. I haven't been much of a churchgoer. No one in my family knows much about the things of God. How can I go to this, Heaven, that I hear about?"

Have you said nearly the same words? Do you have the same question? God, in His great love, wishes to fellowship with the human beings that He has created. This means you. But, human sin separates people from God. So God devised a way for human beings to be forgiven for their sin. He sent His very own Son, Jesus Christ, into the world to die for our sin. His death on the cross-satisfied God's punishment for sin. Jesus was buried for three days and then rose to new life by God's power. Because Christ lives, we can also be resurrected spiritually when we've asked Christ to forgive our sins. We then, need to ask Christ to become a part of our lives. His spirit will come to dwell in our heart for the asking. We will know Christ has answered our prayer because we will have a peace in our heart.

God has prepared a special place for those who have placed their trust in His Son, Jesus. It is called Heaven. The best thing about Heaven is that you are in the presence of the Lord Jesus and God, the Father. There is room for everyone who declares Jesus as Savior. Heaven is a beautiful place filled with love, joy, and peace. We will know our loved ones who have entered Heaven before us. We go to Heaven by believing in Jesus. Won't you bow your head and receive Jesus into Your life today?

Prayer: Dear God, thank You for Jesus taking my punishment for sin. Forgive me my sins. Please come into my life. Grant me Your peace so I know my prayer has been answered. Thank You for the promise of Heaven soon. But, in the meantime, help me live for You, in Jesus' name. Amen.

Come on Home!

"But, seek ye first the kingdom of God, and his righteousness, and all these things shall be added unto you." Matthew 6:33

When you were a child, did you ever have the experience of being caught outside in a fierce storm? It was dark. The wind was blowing and the rain was pelting your face. You began to run but you couldn't see where you were going. Faintly, you heard someone calling your name. Dimly, in the sheets of rain, you saw a light ahead. As you ran toward the voice and the light, the voice became louder. "Come on! Come on home!," you heard in your mother's voice. Again, she called, "Come on!," encouraging you to run through the dark storm to the safety of the warm house.

Sometimes in the journey of life, your way seems dark. Happiness is fleeting. It seems many storms of disappointments and trials have come your way. You've tried to make sense of it all. "What is my purpose in life?" you ask yourself. You seek answers in many places, yet you have no direction. Nothing really satisfies your seeker heart. You long to hear someone calling your name and pointing you to the meaning of life.

May I suggest that you seek God? There may be family members and friends who have already suggested this to you. I invite you to consider the suggestion again. God has the answer for which you are searching. You can look for your answer in the Bible, God's Word, and ask God to reveal to you His truths. Speak to God in prayer. He is always listening day or night. Ask questions of your believing family members, friends, minister or chaplain. As you seek after God and His righteousness, He has promised to fulfill your needs now and forever.

You will find that, as truths are revealed to you, you will want to seek more truth. God honors a seeking heart. Eventually, He calls you to act upon the truths that you have learned with trust. You have to make a commitment to God by asking His Son, Jesus, to forgive your sin and come into your life. God will honor that commitment. The trusting heart will find safety in the heavenly home. Come on home!

Prayer: O God, please reveal Your truth. Help each seeker to accept Your truth and trust in it. Bless each heart with Your promises. Help each seeker to hear the encouraging voice of Your Word and the voice of caring believers. Please guide each seeker toward rest in the safety of Jesus Christ and the heavenly home, in Jesus' name, I pray. Amen.

Be Strong and of Good Courage

"Have I not commanded thee? Be strong and of a good courage; be not afraid, neither be thou dismayed: for the Lord thy God is with thee whithersoever thou goest." Joshua1:9

The unfamiliar and unknown has the potential to cause us to be afraid. In the Bible, the Lord was commanding Joshua to lead his armies into a new land. You see, He promised to go with Joshua wherever he went. When we are afraid or something takes too long, there is a natural tendency to become discouraged. The Lord urges us to be strong and of good courage. He has promised His presence to go with us now and through the doorway of death to Heaven on the other side.

In this instantaneous world, we aren't accustomed to waiting for much of anything. God numbers our days. The number is a mystery to us. When death does not come instantly, some become discouraged. Will they ever receive the promise of God, the reward of Heaven?

It is a sign of strength to wait upon the Lord and be submissive to His will. This is our strength especially when we would rather hasten the inevitable. But, it is an act of obedience to honor the Lord by respecting His timing and His purposes. We are called to trust in the Lord without asking, "Why". Discouragement adds nothing to our witness. May we replace those thoughts with praise to God for the blessings that we have received in the past and in the present. Be strong and of good courage.

Prayer: O Father, forgive me when I let discouragement get the upper hand in my life. Replace these thoughts with an appreciation for Your many blessings. Lead me to honor You in death as well as in life. Help me be submissive to Your will and timing, I pray in Jesus' name. Amen.

Pursue Your Joy

"Rejoice evermore. Pray without ceasing. In every thing give thanks: for this is the will of God in Christ Jesus concerning you." I Thessalonians 5:16-18

What brings you joy? Do visits from family and friends bring you joy? Do painted fingernails or chocolate malts bring you joy? Perhaps, finding a rare stamp for a stamp collection or a new porcelain doll for a doll collection brings you joy. Whatever it is, pursue your joy! Try to give away some joy to others. Showing others appreciation brings them joy. Kind words and compliments lift a weary spirit. There is joy to be found in every day if we will look for it. There are opportunities to receive joy and give joy.

There are opportunities to pray. Perhaps, your fellowship with the Lord in prayer is one of your great joys. Nehemiah 8:10b reminds us ... "neither be ye sorry; for the joy of the Lord is your strength." The Lord loves you today just as much as He did before you became ill. He wants you to be joyful, pray and give thanks. As we do that, we will find strength in our spirit. What is there to be thankful for today? Are you thankful for the medicine that keeps you comfortable? Are you grateful for the Hospice Team that cares for your needs enabling you to stay at home? Are you thankful for such small joys as the sunshine, blooming flowers, bird songs or the laughter of a child? Are you grateful for knowing Christ as your best friend and knowing that He has prepared a heavenly home for you? Today, pursue your joy, pray and give thanks. For this day, it is God's will for you.

Prayer: O Father, thank You for the large and small joys in my life. Help me seek out today's joys. May I bring joy to others. I thank You for my relationship with You. Please, strengthen me in my spirit, in Jesus' name, I pray. Amen.

Are You Cramming for Your Finals?

"Study to shew yourself approved unto God, a workman that needeth not to be ashamed, rightly dividing the word of truth." 2 Timothy 2:15

Do you remember, "cramming for final exams" when you were in school? You diligently studied to pass a test over some content area. Our tests in life are the experiences that challenge us. Yet, God has provided a textbook for us to study to prepare for these tests, the Bible.

As eternity draws closer, do you have questions concerning what the next life will be like? To discover what life is like after death, may I invite you to read the Bible? The Bible is God's Word. It is God's letter to us. While we may not understand everything in the Bible, the Bible gives us answers to the basic questions of life now and life for eternity. Many at eternity's threshold have a hunger for God's Word. They read it or listen to the Bible on a recording. They are anxious to know as much as they can about the next life before they enter that new existence. Knowledge brings security and peace. Yet, if we truly want knowledge revealed to us, we must place our trust in the one who holds all knowledge, Jesus Christ. The Holy Spirit who comes to live in our heart will help us make sense of the Bible and He will help us pass the tests of this life, preparing us for the next. Are you cramming for your finals?

Prayer: 0 God, reveal Your truth to me. Prepare me for eternity with knowledge. Help me allow Your knowledge to bring peace and security to my heart. Let me share these truths with my family, in Jesus' name, Amen.

The First Step of Discipleship

Jesus said, "Go ye therefore, and teach all nations, baptizing them in the name of the Father, and of the Son, and of the Holy Ghost:" Matthew 28:19

Have you been a believer for many years, yet you have not had the opportunity to be baptized? Or, have you recently come to put your trust in Jesus Christ as your Savior and yet you have not taken the first step of discipleship that is baptism? Some churches baptize infants. Then, when these infants come to an age of understanding they confirm or agree with their baptism by making a conscious decision to follow the Lord Jesus. If you were baptized as an infant, have you confirmed that event in your heart? Perhaps, you would like to do so today. Other churches baptize people after they have made a public statement that they believe Jesus is the Son of God and have taken Him as their Savior.

The sacrament of baptism is the outward showing of your commitment of faith in Jesus. Believers' baptism follows confession of faith in the Lord Jesus. Baptism by immersion acts out the Easter story. As the minister immerses you in water, it is as if you are being buried with Christ in the tomb for the penalty of sin. As you rise from the water, it is as if you are being raised to new life in Christ. Jesus has commanded his followers to be baptized. To be baptized in a public service, is the first act of obedience for a Christian. This is an important step to take. It will settle your salvation commitment for you. While you are able, speak to your minister about being baptized. Don't put it off. Following through with this commitment will bring peace to your soul.

You are united by faith to other Christians who become your brothers and sisters in the family of God. May I encourage You to follow through with your commitment to Christ and make plans to take the first step of discipleship that is baptism?

Prayer: Dear Heavenly Father, thank You for Your love for me. Give me the strength to follow You in the first step of obedience that is baptism. Bless my commitment in faith to You, in Jesus' name, I pray. Amen.

The Family Meal

"For I have received of the Lord that which also I delivered unto you, That the Lord Jesus the same night in which he was betrayed took bread? And when he had given thanks, he brake it, and said, Take eat; this is my body, which is broken for you: this do in remembrance of me. After the same manner also he took the cup, when he had supped, saying, This cup is the new testament in my blood: this do ye, as oft as ye drink it, in remembrance of me. For as often as ye eat this bread, and drink this cup, ye do shew the Lord's death till he come." I Corinthians 11:23-26

Perhaps it has been a long time since you were able to attend church and partake in the Lord's Supper. Do you miss the sacrament? Or, has it been so long that you've forgotten what it meant to commune with the Lord and His people around the memorial table? Let me encourage you to ask the leaders of your church to bring Communion to you in your home.

In my experience as a Hospice Chaplain, I have observed that sharing Communion, the family meal of Christians, has comforted my hospice patients. The reading of scripture, prayers and partaking of the elements remind us that Christ gave his all for us on the cross for the forgiveness of our sin. He endured the sting of death out of love for us. Jesus has taken the sting from death for believers. As we share in this family meal, we remember that Christ bought and paid for our eternal life in Heaven. We also are assured that He will come for us to take us home to Heaven one day. Jesus Christ is very present as the host of the Lord's Table. He comforts and sustains us in our spirit. May I encourage you to not neglect the family meal, the Lord's Table, if you are a believer? It is a divine appointment with our Lord to be observed on a regular basis. Jesus said, "This do in remembrance of me." I Cor. 11:24

Prayer: O God, thank You for giving us the sacrament of Communion, the family meal, to help us remember Your great gift of salvation. Please open the opportunity for me to partake in the Lord's Supper during this time. I ask You to forgive my failings and heal my spirit. Please help me remember Your love for me as I take of the bread and cup, in Jesus' name, Amen.

The Gift of Peace

"Peace I leave with you, my peace I give unto you; not as the world giveth, give I unto you. Let not your heart be troubled, neither let it be afraid." John 14:27

Jesus spoke these words. Jesus is still giving his gift of peace to His children today. But, Jesus' gift of peace is different from peace in the world. The world's peace may be the absence of conflict. Jesus' peace is a deep sense of well being in our soul. Our heart needn't be troubled or fearful. Jesus' gift of peace tells us that no matter what, all is well.

For believers in God, we know we have a home in Heaven in Jesus' Presence after our earthly life is over. But, if it pleases the Lord, for us to linger on this earth, we know that the Lord's Presence in our heart will bring us peace.

Peace is given when we need it. The Lord's gift is never a belated present. Yet, as we look ahead, we may worry about coming days. We may not experience peace because the hour of need is not upon us. Jesus is faithful. He promises us the gift of peace. He tells us to not be troubled or afraid. Won't you accept this beautiful gift from the Lord today? He offers you the gift of peace for every need.

Prayer: O God, thank You for Jesus' gift of peace. Quiet my heart right now. Replace my troubled, fearful spirit with Your peace. Thank You that Your peace is equal to every distress. Help me lean on Your everlasting arms, in Jesus' name. Amen.

Is That Your Final Answer, God?

"Is any sick among you? let him call for the elders of the church; and let them pray over him, anointing him with oil in the name of the Lord." James 5:14

Additional Scripture: James 5:13-16

The TV game show host often asks the question, "Is that your final answer?" When the doctor tells you that your body can't get well, you may wonder, "Is that the final answer?" This is a question that needs to be addressed to God in prayer. James, Jesus' half-brother, tells us that if you are sick, you should ask the church leaders to pray for and anoint you with oil in the name of the Lord. The oil represents the Holy Spirit poured upon someone who needs a special healing touch from God.

God is the author of all healing whether it comes by prayer or medicine. When you pray in faith for healing, you must remember that God can respond in different ways. He may grant a physical healing. He may work through doctors and medicine. He may bring you spiritual wholeness and forgiveness but not heal your body. He may restore you to wholeness in His very presence in Heaven. When you pray, it is important for you to seek God's will and be submissive to His will for your life. When you've received Jesus as your Savior, you know your life is His whether you live it on earth or in Heaven. So whether you are present or absent from the body, you are with Jesus. May you find comfort in this truth.

Prayer: Almighty God, You give the final answer to the length of my earthly days. Help me come to You in my need. Forgive my sins, O God. Please, make me spiritually whole. If it is Your will, please heal this body. But, if You have a greater plan for me, help me accept it as coming from Your love; I pray this, in Jesus' name. Amen.

Perfect Wholeness

Matthew 9:20-22: "And, behold, a woman, which was diseased with an issue of blood twelve years, came behind him, and touched the hem of his garment: For she said within herself, If I may but touch his garment, I shall be whole. But Jesus turned him about, and when he saw her, he said, Daughter, be of good comfort; thy faith hath made thee whole. And the woman was made whole from that hour."

God's desire for us is forgiveness and wholeness. His highest priority for us is spiritual wholeness. God answers prayers of faith in many ways. Sometimes in His best plans for us He heals us in the body as He did the woman of the Bible. Sometimes God allows the affliction in the body but His greatest good is to bring healing in the soul, a spiritual healing.

Healing may not always come to us as we expect or wish. While God may not always answer our prayers for physical healing, He will always grant us forgiveness for our shortcomings when we ask for it. This forgiveness will usher in God's best gift to us, perfect wholeness. We can experience this wholeness of the soul now. Our restoration of the soul in this life prepares us for perfect wholeness in the very presence of God.

As a child of God, we have the privilege of asking Him for our heart's desire whatever it may be. Then, we need to trust Him and rest in His choice for our life. While we belong to God because we have trusted our soul to His Son, Jesus, we know that He always makes the best choices for us. God has great purposes for His kingdom in all that

He does. May we glorify His name whether we are present or absent from our body.

Prayer: O God, bring me wholeness. I'll trust You to decide how You do that. Please, accomplish Your best plans for my life even now. Let my life be a witness and praise to Your glory, in Jesus' name. Amen.

A Time to Mourn ...

"To every thing there is a season, and a time to every purpose under the heaven: ...A time to weep, and a time to laugh; a time to mourn, and a time to dance." Ecclesiastes 3:1, 4

There is a time for everything. It is important that we acknowledge our loss and our disappointment that life as we know it is quickly drawing to a close. There is a time to weep in our grief. Yet, not everybody weeps, which is fine. Sometimes sorrow is deeper than tears. Tears are an expression for some of grief, yet there are some who do not express themselves with tears. We express both grief and joy through the unique personality that God gave us. Feelings neither are right nor wrong. They are just feelings.

Although our grief can seem overwhelming and all consuming at times, there is hope. There will be a time to laugh and dance once again. The heavenly home holds no sorrow. The Apostle John speaks these words, "And God shall wipe away all tears from their eyes: and there shall be no more death, neither sorrow, nor crying, neither shall there be any more pain: for the former things are passed away." Revelation 21:4 We have joy to look forward to in the heavenly home.

Even though we will grieve our loss of life coming too soon, we can finish our days by sprinkling them with joy. Let's create shared moments of laughter, shared moments of dancing as well as shared moments of grief with the ones that we love most.

Prayer: O God, I believe there is a time for everything. Help me find strength in sharing my grief with my loved ones. Help me show Your strength as I create moments of laughter and moments of dancing for my loved ones. May Your presence comfort all of us in each of these moments, in Jesus' name, I pray. Amen.

Joy Comes in the Morning

"Weeping may endure for a night, but joy cometh in the morning." Psalm 30:5b

The house is dark and quiet. Everyone is asleep except you. The pain is excruciating. Who can you turn to in the middle of the night? You can turn to God who never sleeps. He is awake all night. Pain gives you an alertness. Medicine often dulls that alertness. It's a trade-off. One time you may desire alertness so you tolerate more pain. Another time you may choose to have less pain and be sleepy to the world. If you have chosen the path of alertness, how do you get through a night of pain?

This is the time to pray to your Heavenly Father. Talk to Him about everything on your heart. Praise Him for your blessings, ask for your needs to be met and pray for others that you know. In the Bible, I Thessalonians 5:17 tells us to, "Pray without ceasing." This is a time to be still and let God speak to your heart and mind. He may do this in several ways. He may bring to your remembrance scriptures. He may show you an image or a picture in your mind. He may put words in your mind that you know are not your own. Keep praying through the pain. As your focus moves to the Lord, after a while the pain may not seem so great. God can carry you through the night and bring joy to you in the morning.

When you have trusted in Jesus as your Savior, your night may be this journey of sickness on earth and your joy will be your rest in the heavenly home.

Prayer: O God, hear my prayers in my night of pain. Please, minister to my need, I pray. Help me serve You even in pain, as I pray for others who sleep while I am awake. Carry me through this night and bring joy in the morning. Help me consistently look forward to the joy of the heavenly home someday, in Jesus' name. Amen.

Encouragers for the Race

"Wherefore seeing we also are compassed about with so great a cloud of witnesses, let us lay aside every weight, and the sin which doth so easily beset us, and let us run with patience the race that is set before us, Looking unto Jesus the author and finisher of our faith; who for the joy that was set before him endured the cross, despising the shame, and is set down at the right hand of the throne of God." Heb. 12:1-2

The legacy that has been left to you by your heroes in your faith and your heroes in your family encourage you in your journey now. These that have gone before you have faced illness, difficulty and disappointment. How have they overcome their challenges emotionally and spiritually? Can you find encouragement in their witness or example?

During this time, many encouragers come your way in the Hospice Team. All at once, you receive visits from nurses, a physical therapist, an occupational therapist, a dietician, your own doctor, a social worker, a pharmacist and a chaplain upon your request. So many new people entering your life may be overwhelming. But, just remember they are your ,"cloud of witnesses", or encouragers cheering you on to the finish line.

Jesus also ran such a race. He could foresee the death that awaited him on the cross for the forgiveness of sins. Yet, He was willing to endure the cross because He could see the joy that it would be to enter Heaven again and sit down at the right hand of the Father. He also looked forward to the joy of His appointed task in this life being completed according to His Father's will. Jesus bought eternal life for all who would trust in Him.

What tasks and purposes have you completed for God? Look forward to God saying to you, "Well done, good and faithful servant." Let your encouragers cheer you on to the finish line. There is much joy set before you.

Prayer: Dear Heavenly Father, I thank You for the witnesses of my heroes of faith and the heroes in my family who have gone to You before me. Teach me from their examples, how to run this race. Let me find a blessing in my encouragers. Please, give me the strength to finish my race well, in Jesus' name. Amen.

I'm Praying for You

"I thank God, whom I serve from my forefathers with pure conscience, that without ceasing I have remembrance of thee in my prayers night and day." 2 Tim. 1:3

Are people telling you that they are praying for you? Is your name spoken for prayer in church? Is your name mentioned on a prayer chain? You may wonder what purpose there is in these prayers.

God is a loving Father. You can ask Him anything that you want. You and others interceding for you may ask for the miracle of physical healing and the miracle of spiritual healing. Prayers may be prayed for you to receive the miracle of inner strength to cope with pain, medication and your own death. Those praying for you may ask that you will be comforted and that you will be at peace. They may ask that all of your needs be met. God works through the prayers of His people. God answers prayers according to His best will for you. He may answer yes, no, or not yet. The pray-er can ask anything but the pray-er must ultimately be willing to trust God enough to accept His answer.

Trust means that you sacrifice what you want to God's choice. You allow Him to have His way. When you trust God with your prayers and the prayers of others, you have peace. You know that however God answers your prayers and the prayers prayed for you; that you will be alright. God will only do the loving thing for you. Leaving the choices up to God will always bring you His best for your life now and His best for your life with Him in Heaven for eternity. Those who place their trust in Christ, as their Savior, cannot lose. God brings His best will to you to accomplish a better life for his child. If you receive a physical healing, your earthly life is good. If you receive a home in Heaven, eternal life is better.

Prayer: O God, I pray for all those reading this devotion. I pray that You would exercise Your best will for each life. I ask that each may know Your love, comfort and ultimate peace. Please continue to bring joy to each person every day. O, God, may You give each person the courage to trust You with their life, in Jesus' name. Amen.

Enveloped in Love

"In my Father's house are many mansions: if it were not so, I would have told you, I go to prepare a place for you. And if I go and prepare a place for you, I will come again, and receive you unto myself; that where I am, there ye may be also." John 14: 2, 3

Love originated with God. God is love. In this world, one of the ways we experience love is in loving our families and being loved by them. In our minds, we can't imagine any love greater than that. This is why it is so hard for us to think about leaving our family to go to Heaven. We want to live in two worlds, the earthly and the heavenly. But, reality is that we can only live in one world at a time.

Allow God's love, which is greater than human love, to draw you to Him. Let Him comfort you and assure you that all will be well. God promises that you will be reunited with your earthly believing loved ones in Heaven. You will be greeted upon your arrival in the heavenly home by loved ones who have entered there before you.

In Heaven, you will not see your loved one's sorrow or struggles on the earth. God in His great love shields us from those hurts because we are not free to minister to those needs as we have before. In Heaven, you will be enveloped in the love and presence of our Lord Jesus Christ. The Lord will be Your shepherd and Your caretaker. You will not want for more. You are moving toward greater love than what you have experienced on earth. May love, peace and contentment be with you.

Prayer: O, Heavenly Father, comfort my heart. It is so hard to say goodbye to loved ones even if it is for a short while. Thank You for the love I have received and have been allowed to give to my family, friends and acquaintances. Please, assure me of Your great love. Help me see that I am coming to greater love than I have ever known, in Jesus' name. Amen.

Don't Put Off 'Till Tomorrow...

"Whereas ye know not what shall be on the morrow. For what is your life? It is even a vapour, that appeareth for a little time, and then vanisheth away. For that ye ought to say, If the Lord will, we shall live, and do this or that." James 4: 14-15

Sometimes it is in dying that you truly learn how to live. You make plans for next week, next month, and next year. Yet, you don't even know what will happen tomorrow. All of us need to look to God as the one who holds our plan book or Day Timer. Let us hold our plans loosely, giving God the privilege of interjecting His own good plans into our lives. What blessings might we miss if we cling only to our own plans?

Can you learn to live in "twenty-four hour" compartments? Can you find joy, sharing, love, forgiveness and friendship in today's moments? Let us not put off conversations, celebrations, visits, times to make peace with others, or moments with God. Perhaps, you feel physically stronger today. Take that shopping trip, go to church, eat pizza out and visit loved ones this day. Make the most of the time you have! Pray that God would lead you into His plans for the present. This is truly the way all of us should live each day of our lives.

Prayer: Dear Heavenly Father, This day I give to You. Help me be present to the people with which I associate. Help me to give good gifts of time, love, sharing and forgiveness to each one. Please, bless this day with Your love, joy and peace, in Jesus' name, I pray. Amen.

The Joys of Today

"This is the day which the Lord hath made; we will rejoice and be glad in it." Psalm 118:24

You've heard it said that yesterday is gone and tomorrow may never come. All any of us really have is today. Today is all that we can really count on. The scriptures guide us into the right attitude that we are to have toward the present. We are to rejoice and be glad in it. Christians know that love, peace, and rest await them in the very presence of the Lord Jesus on the other side of the door of death. So, we needn't fill today with worry. Instead, let us find all the joy in the present and celebrate it.

What little joys can you find today? Perhaps, you will spot a robin as you look out of your window. Maybe, you will see an apple tree bursting forth in bloom. Will you hear a toddler laugh with glee? Will you have a visit from a long time friend? Will you have meaningful conversations with family members? What are your joys today?

You have to name your own joys. Your joys are very individual. Sometimes joys are not always obvious. You have to search for them. Yet, each day has the potential for joy! May you appreciate the blessings that each day brings.

Prayer: Dear Heavenly Father, thank You for this day. Please show me the joy that You have in it for me. Help me appreciate the present. Help me lead others to see the joy in this day and be glad in it, in Jesus' name. Amen.

Occupy Until Jesus Comes

"And he called his ten servants, and delivered them ten pounds, and said unto them, Occupy till I come." Luke 19:13

Just because you are dying, is no reason to stop living too soon. All of us have been aging and moving toward dying since we were born. Although you may be aware that your time for living on the earth is short, you are to occupy till Jesus comes.

Jesus tells a story in the Bible about a ruler taking a business trip to a country far away. He gave money to his servants and told them to put it to work until he returned. Believers in Jesus often interpret this passage for modern days in this way. Jesus has given each of us talents and abilities. He has made an investment in our lives. He wants us to use and multiply the talents that He has given us for His glory.

When you know that Jesus will be coming for you soon, how do you occupy your days? As much as possible, you will probably want to continue sharing your talents and abilities as you have in the past. But, if there has been a life-long desire to accomplish something with your abilities that is yet unfinished, now is the time to do it if you are physically able. If you are not physically able to do the task yourself, perhaps you could teach someone else how to do it. You could encourage and mentor another to carry on the vision that lies in your heart. It is a matter of prayer to find the right person to do that.

Friends that I have met who knew that Jesus was coming for them soon have "occupied" their time in various ways. One cut the pictures off old Christmas cards, fashioned a greeting and recycled them into Christmas postcards to send to family and friends. Another made puff quilts for family members at her sewing machine. Another enjoyed drives to check the cattle and gave farming advice to his farm hands. Whatever your gift, use it as you "occupy" until Jesus comes.

Prayer: Dear Heavenly Father, Help me to "occupy" 'till You come. Give me the strength to use the abilities You have graced me with for Your glory. May these endeavors bring joy, peace and a sense of accomplishment in this season of life, I pray this, in Jesus' name. Amen.

Are You a Forgiver As Well As Forgiven?

"Forbearing one another, and forgiving one another, if any man have a quarrel against any: even as Christ forgave you, so also do ye." Colossians 3:13

Is there someone who has hurt you that you have not forgiven? Is there someone you have hurt but you have not yet asked for their forgiveness? When we refuse to forgive, we want to hold the erring one responsible for their sin. By not forgiving them, we imagine that we are making them "pay" for what they have done. Yet, as a believer is that our judgment to make? Doesn't that judgment belong to the Lord Jesus? Don't we want people to forgive us for our shortcomings? Shouldn't we be willing to extend that same forgiveness to others?

It is part of human nature to fall short of God's best intentions for us. Have you known Christ's forgiveness for your past sins? Have you known the peace that comes into your heart when you've known that He has cleansed you? The Bible teaches us that we are to walk in Christ's footsteps. We are to follow His example. We are even to forgive others as He has forgiven us.

What has been done against us is never the issue. The Apostle Paul tells us in the Bible to forgive whatever grievance we may have against one another. These grievances may range from mild to serious. In the Lord's eyes, they all look the same. Jesus has forgiven each of us of so much. Out of obedience and love for Him, we can do nothing less than to forgive one another. It is vital that we make the effort to reconcile with all those where we recognize there is a grievance in our relationship. May we call that person to us or go to that person. Perhaps, we might write a letter or make a phone call of apology. If our overtures are not accepted, we know we've done the right thing. The responsibility for the grievance is now theirs. May we humble ourselves and clear our accounts with others so that we might enter Heaven as a forgiver as well as forgiven.

Prayer: O God, I have sinned against You in holding onto grievances in my relationships. Forgive me, I pray. Please, give me the strength to forgive others and make peace with them. Help those that I ask forgiveness from, to accept my apologies. Bring peace and reconciliation to my relationships, I pray, in Jesus' name. Amen.

Parenting Children in the Valley of the Shadow of Death

"Train up a child in the way he should go: and when he is old, he will not depart from it." Proverbs 22:6

So you have children, teenagers, not yet ready to make their way in the world. So many days you have so little energy to even talk with your children. But, there are other days when all you want to do is talk to them.

Just because you are dying, you don't cease to be a parent. Perhaps, you have a greater privilege than most parents in teaching your children life's best and important lessons. What lasting lessons do you want to impress upon your teenagers? What have you learned in your life from your experiences that you wish to share with them? What can you tell them about how to choose a mate? What can you tell them about marriage? What can you tell them about raising their own children someday? What does "family" mean to you? What do you have to say about "education"? What can you tell them about faith in God and preparing for a home in Heaven? If you have children too young for these conversations, perhaps you could write or tape record your thoughts to be shared with them when they are old enough to understand your advice.

It may seem like you are fast-forwarding your children's lives at a time when they just want to be kids. Yet you need to make the most of the parenting time that you have. Share your thoughts, your advice, your hopes and dreams for them in short conversations over a period of time. These words of your wisdom will come back to them in their memories to guide them later. Your words may not always be greeted with appreciation now but they will be precious words later in the echoes of your children's memories.

Prayer: O God, guide me in what to teach my children about life. Please, give me the words that will be memorable. Help me put my words in the right order so that my children may grasp them and hold them in their hearts. O God, call these words forth when my children need them and help them apply them to their lives, I pray these things, in Jesus' name. Amen.

Finishing Business

"My times are in thy hand." Psalm 31:15a

Our times are in the hand of God. Doctors can estimate when our life will begin and how long our life may last based on statistics. But, even they really don't know the day, the hour, or the minute, life as we know it, on earth will cease. Our times truly are in the hand of the Almighty Creator.

So how do you handle the time you have, when you learn it could be shorter than you had expected? Do you make the best use of the time? What do you need to do to finish up business with your loved ones? It is so often a comfort to families to know the wishes of the one dying for funeral and memorial arrangements. If your family has not yet faced this reality and cannot hear your words, you might consider writing your wishes in a notebook to be read by them when needed. Or, this may be the time for you to bring up a conversation with your spouse and children of any wishes for the future that you would like for them to carry out. Now is the opportunity to discuss and make family decisions concerning what measures you want or don't want to sustain your earthly life. Do you need to put your business affairs in order? None of these steps are easy to take. But, preparing your family for the days ahead is a loving gift that you can give them. When your family knows your wishes, they are much more at peace with carrying out those wishes because they feel they are honoring your memory by respecting your wishes. Even in times such as these, you can guide your family concerning your wishes. It is a gift of love.

Prayer: O God, I acknowledge my time is in Your hand. I trust You to measure my days rightly in Your best plan. Please, guide me in sharing my wishes with loved ones. Help me have the words to say and the courage to say them. Show me how to do what I can to make the journey easier for my family after I move to Heaven. May I give this gift of love and peace to my loved ones, in Jesus' name, I pray. Amen.

Everyday Pleasures

"The Lord is my strength and song, and is become my salvation." Psalm 118:14

What "everyday" pleasures do you include in your life? Do you like to fish? Go fishing. Do you like to have your fingernails painted? Then, paint your fingernails or have someone else do it for you. Do you like to create your own gifts for others? Get a head start on the Christmas season by beginning today. Do you like to go to the Dairy Sweet for an ice cream cone? Please go. Do you have a collection - stamps, rocks or dolls? Continue to add to that collection or send your children on a hunt and find mission for additions.

Illness has brought many changes to your normal routine. But, illness doesn't have to destroy all your pleasures! Enjoy the "everyday" things that you can. There is comfort in keeping some of these "everyday" pleasures as a part of your life. They bring a sense of normalcy to a very changeable time.

Besides these pleasures, keep your devotional routines. Spend time in prayer. If you can read the scriptures, do so. If that is too taxing, family members or friends might read to you. You might choose to listen to recorded scriptures. Do the old hymns bring you comfort? Or, does more contemporary music minister to your soul? Music is very soothing. Listen often.

Don't be afraid to start a new routine or add a new pleasure. Perhaps, you never liked anything with strawberries in it and now you love strawberry smoothies. Good for you! It is so tempting to draw inward in times like these. But, it is in times like these that your loved ones most want to connect with you. Can you share an "everyday pleasure" with them? It will help them as much as it will help you. Let God be your strength and your song.

Prayer: O God, Thank You for the "everyday" pleasures of life. Please, give me the strength to share them with my loved ones. Thank You for the comfort there is in the everyday spiritual routines. May Your presence and Your people surround me each day until I meet You face to face, in Jesus' name. Amen.

Giving Your Gifts

"Freely you have received, freely give." Matthew 10:8 Do you like to give gifts? Does it give you pleasure to see delight in another's face over a gift received? You have a unique opportunity during this time to give gifts to your family and friends. These may be treasures you have cherished over the years. They might have great sentimental value. Or, they might be very practical gifts that fill needs in the lives of others. Some gifts may just bring beauty to the receiver in the form of a poem, a painting, a crocheted doily, or a handcrafted wooden item etc. Can you match the gift to the receiver blessing their lives? What gifts of wisdom, godly advice, and experiences with the Lord could you use with which to encourage others? What mentoring do you need to do for someone looking up to you?

Giving will bring you joy. It will bless the life of a loved one. The gift is also a reminder of you to the receiver. They will think about the good memories of time spent with you every time they look at your gift. This can be healing to the receiver in the days to come.

Not everyone has the opportunity to plan "gifts of the heart" for those they love. If this would be healing for you to give gifts to your loved ones, begin planning them now. Enlist help from others to accomplish this. Acts 10:35b reminds us, "It is more blessed to give than to receive."

Prayer: O God, thank You for all with which You have blessed me. Now, help me bring joy to others by giving gifts of my treasures. Bless each receiver. May each gift commemorate my love for each person, in Jesus' name, I pray. Amen.

Building Your Legacy

"Fervent in spirit; serving the Lord." Romans 12:11

You are in a unique position to minister to others and serve the Lord even in this season of life. What have you learned about God, about life, and about relationships with others that you feel is worthy to pass on? What of your gifts and talents can you still use to communicate the life lessons that build your legacy?

Perhaps, you may want to tell all those you encounter, to build good memories so that those memories will warm them in this season. Maybe, you will want to tell them that the sharing of love with family and friends is very important in this life. Perhaps, you will want to share your faith in God and in how others can trust Him, too. Maybe your gift will be teaching others how to handle the end of their earthly life with peace and grace. Those around you will "catch" your perspective and will be able to deal with your death as you have done. Yes, even from your bed, God may call you to lead others to greater understanding of His ways.

God has gifted you through your life with gifts to be used for Him. Even now, use those gifts of drawing, painting, composing songs, composing poems, quilting, woodworking and so forth to communicate life lessons to others that may light their way in the journey of life. For those who have led a very active life, understand that while some activities are beyond your grasp, there are things you can do to serve the Lord in another dimension. Pray that the Lord will show you how to serve others at this time. The Lord will bring you people from your past, your present and new friends in this season. Build your legacy by ministering to them in the name of the Lord.

Prayer: Dear Heavenly Father, May I magnify You to all who come to my bedside. Give me the words to speak, the drawings to draw, the poems to write, the songs to sing, the quilts to make, the wood to carve and so forth to package the life lessons You have taught me so they may be readily reviewed. Please, give me the courage to share them in the short time that I have. Help me to use my time well for You, God. May the legacy I leave enrich the lives of those I touch, in Jesus' name, I pray. Amen.

To be Present with the Lord

"Therefore we are always confident, knowing that whilst we are at home in the body, we are absent from the Lord: (For we walk by faith, not by sight;) We are confident, I say, and willing rather to be absent from the body, and to be present with the Lord." 2 Corinthians 5:6-8

When you are walking outside on a beautiful sunny spring day, what do you do when you get too warm? Don't you take your jacket off because you don't need it anymore?

I Corinthians 15:50 in the Bible tells us in the Apostle Paul's words, "Now this I say brethren, that flesh and blood cannot inherit the kingdom of God..." Paul is saying that our bodies of flesh and blood cannot enter Heaven. We will take off our body on moving day just like we removed our jacket on a warm afternoon because we won't need it anymore. It is our soul that will go to be with the Lord Jesus immediately if we have trusted Him as our Savior. Death is the separation of the soul from the body. Our soul enters the heavenly home.

One day when Jesus returns to earth in His Second Coming, He will raise our bodies and change them into spiritual bodies fit for Heaven. At that time, our new spiritual bodies will be reunited with our souls that have been with Jesus. To be absent from the body of our flesh that suffers so much is to be present with the Lord. In Jesus' presence, there is love, hope and peace. All pain and suffering is finished. Could there really be a better place to be than in the presence of the Lord?

Prayer: O God, thank You for Your promise that to be absent from the body is to be in Your presence in the heavenly home. Help me look forward to being in Your presence and knowing Your love, hope and peace in new ways, in Jesus' name, I pray. Amen.

Family Reunion

"For now we see through a glass, darkly; but then face to face: now I know in part; but then shall I know even as also I am known."
I Corinthians 13:12

People often wonder, "Will I know my believing family members and friends in Heaven?" The answer is, "Yes!" Although flesh and blood cannot inherit Heaven, every soul that enters Heaven will be clothed with a new resurrection body at Christ's Second Coming. We don't know exactly how we will know each other but there will be a likeness in body or in spirit to our earthly person that will be recognized. Now, we don't know all the details of recognizing our loved ones in Heaven. But, the scripture verse assures us that we will fully know others just as they will fully know us.

In other words, we will recognize others just as they will recognize us. What a wonderful thing it is to look forward to being reunited with spouses, parents, brothers, sisters, grandparents and friends! The love that you've shared with them will continue in the Heavenly Home. In Heaven, we will all live together as brothers and sisters. We will not marry or be married because marriage is an institution for earth only for the purpose of establishing the family. Yet, to be in the presence once again of loved ones in Heaven is a beautiful gift. May we find comfort in this hope.

Prayer: Dear Heavenly Father, thanks for the gift of reuniting believing family members and friends in Heaven. We are grateful for the knowledge that we will recognize loved ones and we will be recognized there. Comfort us with this hope, in Jesus' name, I pray, Amen.

Crossing Time

"We are confident, I say, and willing rather to be absent from the body, and to be present with the Lord." 2 Corinthians 5:8

Blink your eyes. This is how long it will take for the believer's soul to cross over from the body to be at home with the Lord. It will only be a moment when crossing time comes. When you take your last breath on earth, the very next moment your soul will be in the very presence of the Lord Jesus Christ.

Isn't that comforting? One moment you are on earth, the next in Heaven. It is as quick as the blink of an eye.

All those who have trusted in Christ Jesus as their Savior will experience this crossing over into the heavenly home. This experience can be described as like the experience of a little child falling asleep on the couch in front of the TV. The father carries the child to his bedroom. The child may rouse finding himself at home in his own room. Many have found comfort in the thought that crossing time will be as quick as a blink of an eye. To be reunited with the Lord Jesus Christ is the ultimate goal of the spiritual life at "crossing time".

Prayer: O God, I thank You that when Jesus Christ is my Savior, I can be victorious over death. Praise You for making the "crossing time" quick as the blink of an eye. Comfort my heart with the thought. Help me look forward to crossing into Your presence, in Jesus' name. Amen.

Your Entrance to Heaven

"For so an entrance shall be ministered unto your abundantly into the everlasting kingdom of our Lord and Saviour Jesus Christ." 2 Peter 1:11

Do you remember as a child waiting for relatives to arrive at your house for the annual family reunion? Remember watching at the window in anticipation that the next car would hold your favorite aunt or uncle? Think about how excited you were to see relatives that perhaps you had not seen in a long time?

Can you imagine that a similar scene is taking place in Heaven on your arrival day? Loved ones already in the heavenly home may be watching for you to arrive in excited anticipation! The angels will be anticipating your arrival with joy. But, most of all, Jesus Christ is lovingly and gently drawing you to Him. He wants to welcome you with love, comfort and peace.

In this world, when kings and presidents arrive at summit meetings, an entrance is prepared for them complete with people standing, people clapping and the playing of a musical fanfare. The Apostle Peter says that, "an entrance shall be ministered unto you abundantly." There is a very fine welcome an – "entrance" - being prepared for you on your arrival day into the everlasting heavenly home. May your heart be comforted.

Prayer: O God, thank You for those loved ones awaiting me in Your heavenly home. Most of all, thank You for Your presence and for Your Son, Jesus Christ in Heaven. Comfort my heart and still my anxieties about arrival day. I place my trust in You, in Jesus' name. Amen.